SCIENTISTS AND THEIR DISCOVERIES
GALILEO

SCIENTISTS AND THEIR DISCOVERIES

ALBERT EINSTEIN

ALEXANDER FLEMING

ALFRED NOBEL

BENJAMIN FRANKLIN

CHARLES DARWIN

GALILEO

GREGOR MENDEL

ISAAC NEWTON

LEONARDO DA VINCI

LOUIS PASTEUR

THOMAS EDISON

SCIENTISTS AND THEIR DISCOVERIES
GALILEO

MARY STEFFANELLI

MASON CREST

Mason Crest
450 Parkway Drive, Suite D
Broomall, Pennsylvania 19008
(866) MCP-BOOK (toll-free)
www.masoncrest.com

Printed and bound in the United States of America.

CPSIA Compliance Information: Batch #SG2018.
For further information, contact Mason Crest at 1-866-MCP-Book.

First printing
9 8 7 6 5 4 3 2 1

Library of Congress Cataloging-in-Publication Data on file with the Library of Congress

ISBN: 978-1-4222-4029-8 (hc)
ISBN: 978-1-4222-7761-4 (ebook)

Scientists and their Discoveries series ISBN: 978-1-4222-4023-6

Developed and Produced by National Highlights Inc.
Interior and cover design: Yolanda Van Cooten
Production: Michelle Luke

CONTENTS

KEY ICONS TO LOOK FOR:

 Words to understand: These words with their easy-to-understand definitions will increase the reader's understanding of the text while building vocabulary skills.

 Sidebars: This boxed material within the main text allows readers to build knowledge, gain insights, explore possibilities, and broaden their perspectives by weaving together additional information to provide realistic and holistic perspectives.

 Educational videos: Readers can view videos by scanning our QR codes, providing them with additional educational content to supplement the text. Examples include news coverage, moments in history, speeches, iconic sports moments, and much more!

 Text-dependent questions: These questions send the reader back to the text for more careful attention to the evidence presented there.

 Research projects: Readers are pointed toward areas of further inquiry connected to each chapter. Suggestions are provided for projects that encourage deeper research and analysis.

 Series glossary of key terms: This back-of-the-book glossary contains terminology used throughout the series. Words found here increase the reader's ability to read and comprehend higher-level books and articles in this field.

Galileo demonstrates the power of his improved telescope to Venetian leaders in St Mark's Square.

WORDS TO UNDERSTAND

concave lens—a lens in which one or both sides curve inward. The edges are thicker than the center. Rays of light are spread out after passing through it.

convex lens—a lens in which one or both sides curve outward. The center of the lens is thicker than the edges. Rays of light converge on each other after passing through such a lens.

Holy Inquisition—an institution of the Roman Catholic Church, founded to punish those who defied the teachings of the Church.

philosophy—the word means, literally, "the love of wisdom." It has come to mean the study of events and actions from the point of view of their underlying causes and reasons.

theology—the science dealing with God's relation to man and the universe, based on faith and information revealed in the scriptures.

CHAPTER 1

Seeing More Clearly

Early in 1609, rumors began circulating around Europe of a new and marvelous instrument. A Flemish optician had, it seemed, "found the art of seeing far places and things as if nearby." The news spread quickly. In April, "glasses of a new invention" had reached Paris and, by May, as far as Milan. Spectacle-makers tried to discover the "secret" for themselves.

At the end of July there was news that the Flemish optician was on his way to Venice. He was bringing a "perspective glass" with him, hoping to sell it to the authorities for a large sum of money. That man was possibly Hans Lippershey, from Middleburg in Flanders (present-day Belgium). Although no one will ever be quite sure, he is often credited as the inventor of the first useful telescope.

Visiting Venice at that time was a middle-aged professor of mathematics from Padua University named Galileo Galilei. He was a short, stocky man with red hair, who at the time was concerned with the laws of motion. But when he heard of the arrival in Italy of that "certain Fleming," and of what he was bringing with him, his imagination was fired. He rushed from Venice to intercept the man and find out more about his "spyglass," but they never met.

When Galileo returned to Padua, he worked out the principles for himself. It took him a single day. He made a telescope and, more importantly, he discovered the optical principles upon which it worked. He used a combination of a weak **convex lens** and a strong **concave lens**. This arrangement is now known as the "Galilean" type of telescope.

For a short video on Galileo and his telescope, scan here:

The Venetian authorities did not buy Lippershey's instrument. Instead, Galileo presented them with one of his own. It was far superior to Lippershey's in power and quality. From the tower in St Mark's Square, ships could be seen heading for the port of Venice two hours before they were visible to the naked eye.

Galileo was soon pointing his telescope upward, toward the stars. His astronomical discoveries made him famous all over Europe. But those discoveries, and his interpretations of them, ultimately led to persecution by the Roman Catholic Church. His scientific theories put him in opposition to a **philosophy** of nature that was accepted almost without question. That philosophy had remained intact for almost 2,000 years.

Galileo was a distinguished scientist—a "mathematician and philosopher," as he liked to call himself. He wrote and argued about his ideas. He talked of his experiments much as scientists do today. Why, then, was he treated so harshly?

A Revival of the Ancients

By the end of the 1500s, science had not yet shown itself to be useful in expanding our knowledge of the world. Galileo was to prove to be one of the pioneers of the movement that gave science the credibility it now enjoys.

A statue of Galileo Galilei holding his telescope outside of the Uffizi, a museum in Florence, Italy, that was once the headquarters of the powerful Medici family.

LEARNING IN THE MEDIEVAL WORLD

After the fall of the western Roman Empire in 476 CE, Europe gradually entered a period of economic and intellectual decline. Various invading forces attacked and pillaged schools and libraries, and much ancient learning was lost.

Beginning in the eleventh century CE, European Christians waged a series of wars, called the Crusades, against Arab Muslims for control over Jerusalem and other important areas of the Middle East. As the Europeans conquered territory, scholars began bringing large quantities of manuscripts to Europe. Among them were Arabic editions of ancient Greek books: the work of such men as Galen, Ptolemy, Euclid, Archimedes, and, most importantly, Aristotle. These works were translated into Latin, the language of educated Europeans, and scholars throughout the continent began to study the ideas and knowledge of the ancient philosophers. They were overwhelmed by their insights into the natural world. This ancient knowledge would dominate European scholarship for 500 years.

Some of this ancient knowledge was thought to contradict the Christian scriptures. But, thanks to translations and commentaries by such churchmen as Saint Thomas Aquinas during the thirteenth century, explanations were created to resolve some of these conflicts. Soon, nearly all of the ancient Greeks' work—particularly that of Aristotle—began to be blended with Christian belief. To argue against Aristotle was to argue against God's view of the world as expressed in the Bible.

Galileo was born toward the end of this period, and grew up in this climate of reverence for Greek thought.

But, in the centuries before Galileo, a lot had already happened. The first universities in Europe had been established in the early thirteenth century. They preached a new system of thought, argument, and education. Christian monasteries in Europe, where books had previously been kept, had been centered around the value of an inward-looking, devotional life, but the universities were centers for the inquiring mind—and they found plenty to do.

After the medieval period, Italy became the source and center of the artistic and cultural flowering known as the Renaissance. At the end of the sixteenth century, Italy held an important position in Europe. At the time, the area that today is known as Italy was not one nation, but seven separate and independent city-states.

For the Roman Catholic Church, however, the sixteenth century was a time of crisis. Men like Martin Luther, John Calvin, and John Knox were repelled by the corruption and the excesses that had crept into the Church of Rome. They led a movement to return the Church to a purer, simpler faith. This Protestant Reformation had inspired some European rulers to break away from the authority of Rome. Leaders of the Catholic Church tried to stop this division of the faithful. A Church institution known as the **Holy Inquisition** was strengthened to deal with heresy—any teachings that contradicted the beliefs of the Catholic Church.

In Europe, the universities were rather set in their ways. They absorbed the knowledge of ancient thinkers, but the university scholars rarely tried to go further. University education promoted reasoning rather than experiment. The standard curriculum was to blame for this. Universities were established to provide an education for the mind, focusing on three areas: law, philosophy, and **theology**. The disciplines that we understand as sciences today, such as physics, did not yet exist; they were considered a branch of philosophy.

Although students had numerous books about the teachings of Aristotle and other ancient thinkers, the theories of Aristotle and the others were rarely tested. For example, no one ever bothered to challenge Aristotle's proposal that objects with different weights would fall to Earth at different speeds. To the university scholars, the purpose for study was to find a cause or reason for things being as they were. Experimentation and testing of theories was scorned for showing only the effects of things—the "how," not the "why." But human reasoning and debate could not always give accurate answers. Fourteenth-century French astronomer Nicole Oresme said that reason was not enough to prove whether the Earth moved or stood still. Ultimately, before Galileo, most people went back to the authoritative books of the ancient philosophers to find their answers.

But changes were happening. There were signs of a new step forward. Doctors and anatomists at Padua were starting to question the observations of the Greek authority on medicine, Galen. Some of Aristotle's ideas about motion were coming under scrutiny. And, in the theory of music, experiments were showing that Pythagoras's mathematical basis of harmony did not match what was actually heard. Galileo's own father, Vincenzio, was a key figure in this field, and he carried out many experiments on musical harmony.

The Early Years

Galileo Galilei, the oldest of seven children, was born in Pisa on February 15, 1564. As a child, he was immensely interested in music. He became a brilliant lute player and adored poetry and literature all his life.

However, Vincenzio Galilei wanted his eldest son to study medicine, and so in 1581 Galileo enrolled at the University of Pisa. But he discovered the delights of mathematics rather than medicine. When his father heard that Galileo was likely to fail his exams, he was very concerned. A doctor could find a well-paid position anywhere, but where could a mathematician go? Galileo enjoyed the geometry of Euclid and the way that Archimedes applied his mathematics to

Opposite page: During Galileo's lifetime, Europe looked very different than it does today, as the modern boundaries of nations had not yet been established. The region that today includes the country of Italy was made up of many small kingdoms, including the Duchy of Tuscany, based in Florence and ruled by the Medici family. Other powerful city-states included Venice, Parma, and Milan. Lands ruled by the Roman Catholic Church were known as the Papal States.

ITALY

at the end of the

SIXTEENTH CENTURY

English Miles

Galileo enrolled at the University of Pisa, but was unable to complete his studies there.

problems in physics. They were to become his heroes, and were the only ancient thinkers for whom he later felt any respect.

As his father had feared, Galileo left the University of Pisa in 1585 without a medical degree and without a job. He taught mathematics privately to anyone willing to pay. Eventually, the Marquis Guidobaldo del Monte, himself a great writer on mechanics, used his influence on Galileo's behalf. In 1589, at the age of twenty-five, Galileo started his scientific career as Professor of Mathematics at his former university.

At Pisa, Galileo showed a fascination with the laws of motion. An unpublished book by him about motion still survives in manuscript form. Two well-known stories date from his time there. During the church services one evening, Galileo is said to have watched the movement of a chandelier in the cathedral. He began to time the swings by his pulse. He noticed that the chandelier always took exactly the same time to swing from one side that it took to swing to the other. Another story that Galileo's assistant told many years later was about his experiment of dropping two weights from

Statue of the Greek mathematician Archimedes (ca. 287–212 BCE). He is most remembered for his discovery of the "Archimedes Principle" of bodies in water, and for his machines of war.

the Leaning Tower of Pisa. The heavier weight did not fall faster, as common sense (and Aristotle) suggested. Both stories have become part of the "myth" of Galileo, but they are probably true. He already possessed a keen sense of observation and experiment.

But his stay at Pisa was not a success. He intensely disliked the way his colleagues defended the authorities—the Bible and Aristotle—no matter what their own observations and evidence indicated. To him they were "philosophizing not with due circumspection but merely from having memorized a few ill-understood principles." He became estranged from many of the other professors. In 1592 he moved to the freer atmosphere of the University of Padua. Again, he was Professor of Mathematics, but at three times his previous salary. Galileo welcomed the change, and he stayed at Padua for eighteen years.

During these years, he did his most important work on the laws of motion. He wrote on mechanics and he became concerned with technological problems—fortifications, canals, and gunnery. In 1594 he patented a type of water pump, and in 1597 he devised a "sector," an ingenious instrument used as a calculating aid for gunners. Versions of the sector were used well into the nineteenth century.

Galileo was beginning to show his potential.

Opposite page: Galileo in the cathedral at Pisa. His discovery of the properties of the pendulum are said to date from watching the swing of the chandelier.

The Reformation, which began as a movement to curb abuses by powerful clergy of the Roman Catholic Church, resulted in more than a century of warfare in Europe. This sixteenth-century woodcut shows Roman Catholic troops attacking a Protestant fortress in Maastricht (now the Netherlands).

TEXT-DEPENDENT QUESTIONS

1. Who is credited as the inventor of the first useful telescope?
2. What did Christian scholars bring back from lands reconquered from Arabs during the Crusades that would affect the scientific view of the world?
3. Where was Galileo Galilei born?
4. How did Galileo support himself after leaving the University of Pisa?

RESEARCH PROJECT

Hans Lippershey is often credited as the inventor of the first useful telescope, but there are several other possible candidates for this accomplishment. Read about the history of the telescope, and prepare a presentation for your class. Use evidence that you find in library books or on the internet to support your conclusion about who may have created the first telescope.

Statue of the Greek philosopher Aristotle (384–322 BCE) in a public square in Thessaloniki, Greece. His observations of nature and his ideas about the workings of the universe were not seriously challenged until the sixteenth century.

 WORDS TO UNDERSTAND

centrifugal force—the outward force felt by an object rotating in a circle around a fixed point. Centrifugal means, literally, "center fleeing."

cosmology—the science of the origin and structure of the universe, and of the laws governing it. Also, a theory devised to explain the origin and structure of the universe.

geocentric—a cosmology in which the Earth is thought of as being in the center. The Ptolemaic and Tychonic theories of the universe are geocentric systems.

heliocentric—a cosmology in which the sun is thought of as being in the center. The Copernican system is an example.

parallax—a change in the apparent position of a star due to a change in the position of the observer. In astronomy, for example, it can mean the difference in the direction of a star as seen from different points on the Earth, or from different points on its orbit around the sun. This apparent change in position can be seen as a change in position of that star against the background of more distant stars.

supernova—the sudden and very violent explosion of a star brought about by its collapse after it has run out of hydrogen fuel.

CHAPTER 2

An Earth-Centered Universe

At Padua, Galileo showed more interest in mechanics than in astronomy. But in 1597, he wrote to German astronomer and mathematician Johannes Kepler. Galileo wrote that he, like Kepler, believed that the Earth was not motionless at the center of the universe as was generally thought. Instead, he believed in the theory of Polish astronomer Copernicus (1473–1543). "Copernicus," wrote Galileo, "is yet by an infinite number (for such is the multitude of fools) laughed at and rejected."

Galileo dared not admit this openly. The Roman Catholic Church did not share Copernicus's belief that the sun, rather than the Earth, was at the center of the universe. Galileo was far too close to Rome, the center of the Catholic Church, to challenge its doctrines.

Galileo had grown up with a **cosmology**, or theory of the universe, very different from our own. Although all astronomers accepted that the Earth was round, most believed that it was located at the center of the universe and was quite still. They believed that it neither rotated on its axis, nor revolved around the sun. Instead, the cosmology of Galileo's time placed the Earth at the center of a nest of transparent spheres. Locked in these spheres, the sun, moon, and planets revolved around the Earth. Beyond Saturn, the outermost planet then known, was the vast sphere of the stars, turning every twenty-four hours and turning the spheres of the planets within it. Beyond this final sphere was the infinite realm of the angels overseeing the whole play of the universe. It was a beautiful system. It agreed with common sense, astronomy and theology, and it had remained substantially unchanged for 1,500 years.

The Geocentric Universe

Philosophers had given good reasons why the Earth should be motionless at the center of things. That the Earth stayed still was obvious—we feel no movement beneath our feet. Also, if the Earth rotated about its axis, it seemed obvious that everything would be thrown off into the sky by the **centrifugal force**, like stones from a sling. If the Earth rotated about the sun, astronomers would have detected changes in the brightness and positions of the stars as the Earth swung closer to one side of the starry sphere, and then away again as the year progressed. No such changes, or **parallax**, had been detected.

Until Galileo's time, these commonsense arguments could not be answered. There was "evidence" from the Bible too. Many passages can be quoted to support this cosmology. A committee of theologians declared in 1616 that the idea that the Earth moved around the sun and on its own axis was "foolish and absurd ... it expressly contradicts the doctrine of the Holy Scriptures in many passages."

Aristotle (384–322 BCE) had given this **geocentric** (Earth-centered) universe its basic form. Aristotle had other reasons why the Earth had to be at the center. He believed all matter in the world to be made up of combinations of four basic elements. Their only similarity with modern chemical elements was that they were originally thought to be the basic building blocks of all matter. Aristotle's elements of earth, water, air, and fire are roughly equivalent to our concepts of solid, liquid, gas, and heat.

Each element had a "natural motion." If left to themselves, fire and air were seen to rise, water and earthy matter to fall. The elements had "heaviness" or "lightness." The seas, being less heavy than earthy matter, lay on top of it. Flames, being lighter than air, reached upward through it. Aristotle was always concerned with why things happened. He said that this "natural motion" up or down was a sign that all matter was trying to reach its "natural place" in the universe. When an apple fell from a tree, it was merely fulfilling its "natural tendency" to go

ter moueť: ac ſcðm diſpoſitionem diuerſam materie apparet diuerſimode. Cum enim cometa in medio eſt groſſioꝛis ſubſtantie ꞇ in ertremis ptib⁹ ſubtilioꝛis: tñc i medio apparet lumeñ magⁱ opaciⁱ: ꞇ i ertremis magis clariⁱ:ꞇ vocaʈ ſtella comata:ſed qñ illa materia ertendiʈ i longuⁱ:vocaʈ caudata:ꞇ qñ bʒ ptes ſubtiles inferi⁹ vocaʈ barbata. Et ſic pʒ cᷘ cometa e̅ erhalatio terreſtrⁱ calida ꞇ ſicca:groſſa piguis ꞇ viſcoſa:cui⁹ ptes multi adinuicⁱ circuⁱiaceʈ: eleuata ab iſtⁱ iferioribꝰ vſꝗ ad ſuprmⁱ regioᷓeʒ aerꝯ,in ꝗ ꝗ motu illⁱ regioᷓis iflⁱamaʈ.ꞇ circulariʈ moueť.

Etiⁱ pʒ cᷘ cometa fi̅ multi ghⁱaʈ i byeme ppter multⁱ frigiditateʒ. Nec i eſtate ppter nimiⁱ caliditate.ſʒ bñ in Autⁱno ꞇ in vere. Wiñꝰ tñ in ve: ppter nimiⁱ frigiditateʒ Pʒ eʈ ppter ꝗd cometa tⁱ diu duraʈ ꞇ vñ puenit diuerſitas coloꝛ. Duraʈ eñ diu ppť groſſitiⁱ materie: ꞇ qꞁ ꝉtinuⁱ noua attrabiʈ materia:ꝗ qñ eſt bñ iflⁱamabilis apparet cometa albꝰ vel pallidꝰ:qñ ꝟo e̅ mediocris apparet cometa rubeꝰ:ꞇ qñ e̅ croceꝰ appet vt carbo ardēs. Vñ cometa e̅ ſignⁱ multoꝛ ꝓ10 ei eſt ſignⁱ magne caliditat̅ ꞇ multoꝛ vētoꝛ.Sꝉdo eſt ſignⁱ traditioñⁱ:moꝛtalitatuʒ:belloꝛ:ꞇ peſtⁱ: qꞁ tpe ghⁱatiōis comete viget caliditas ignea:ꞇ caloꝛ i boibꝰ multiⁱ augeʈ.ꞇ etiⁱ coleraⁱ:ꞇ ſic icitaͮʈ boies ad iurgia ꞇ bella. Tertio e̅ ſignⁱ moꝛtalitaťͣ ꝓnciⁱ piꞁ:qꞁ ꝓncipes delicaťͣ viuⁱť:ꞇ ið citⁱ iflⁱamantur. Et ſi ghⁱaʈ cuiⁱ nature e̅ cometa. Dr̅ cᷘ eſt nature calideꞁ ſicce.Qð pʒ.Lⁱ ꝓ10:qꞁ tñc e̅ magna ſiccitas qñ cometa apparet.Cum ſcðo: qꞁ tñc e̅ multitudo magnoꝛ vētoꝛ. Jtē eſt ertpⁱti cᷘ cñ appuit cometa ſicca: fuiʈ byēs ꞇ vēťͣ boꝛealis. Jtē etiⁱ tpe comete i egyptijs fluuijs cecidit lapis err̅e a vēto eleuaťͣ Jtē ſub ꝓncipe.Nicomacho factus fuiʈ cometes circa eꝗnoctialem circulⁱʒ: qⁱ a veſpa faciⁱs oꝛťͣ paucis diebꝰ durauiʈ:ꞇ tñc vehemēs vēʈ.Coꝛinthⁱ verauiʈ igitur cometa eſt nature calide ꞇ ſicce

De galacia ſeu via lactea.

galacia direrⁱt ⁱtiꝗ cᷘ ſol ſemel duⁱ cⁱꞇ a phetᷓte errⁱit vⁱa ſuⁱ: ꞇ non recte durⁱit curⁱi ſuⁱ:ꞇ ið cöbuſſit illⁱ ꝓ teʒ qⁱ nꞁc videʈ alba:ꞇ ðⁱ via lactea Et hec opio eſt pithagoꝛicoꝛ. Jꝑa tñ eſt falſa et friuola.Lⁱ ꝓ1o:qꞁ zodiacⁱ ſub quo moueʈ ſol iam e̅ꝯ combuſťͣ qð eſt falſuⁱ. Sed

anarⁱagoꝛas ꞇ demⁱocritꝰ direrⁱt galaciⁱ cᷘ lumen quoꝛⁱdⁱ aſtroꝛ aggregatoꝛ.Et non videʈ tale lumen de die: qꞁ obfuſcatur a ſole. Sʒ hec opio eſt falſa:qꞁ tñc galacia aliꞁ qñ deberet appere circa aliquas ſtellas: et aliqñ circa alias:qñ ſicuʈ ſol: nꞁc iſtas:nꞁc illas ſtellas obfuſcat. Jtem celum eſt maiꝰ magnitudiⁱe terre: ergo terra nð impedit qñ interpðiʈ inter ſolⁱ ꞇ illa aſtra qñ illuminet illa aſtra. Alij ꝟo direrⁱt cᷘ lumⁱe aſtroꝛ immiſceʈ vapoꝛi bⁱido ꞇ reflectiʈ ad celuⁱ:ꞇ ſic galacia e̅ lumⁱe refleruⁱ ab aere vel coꝛpe bⁱido vſꝗ ad celuⁱ. Sʒ hec opio falſa eſt: qꞁ galacia ſꝑ deberet apparere in alio et alio loco:qð eſt ꝓtra erperientia. Jtē galacia ꝓt appere denocte in aꝗ vel iⁱ ſpeculo. ꞇ tñ tñc nð fit reflerioⁱ vſꝗ ad celuⁱ igⁱ. Jð dicendⁱ eſt cᷘ galacia eſt lumen aſtroꝛ rece ptⁱ in erhalationibꝰ calidis ꞇ ſiccis eleuaťͣ ꝓ caloꝛem ſolis ab iſtis inferioꝛibꝰ vſꝗ ad ſuprmam regionⁱ aerꝯ. Pꝛobaʈ.Lⁱ ꝓ1 mo:qꞁ ꝓ virtutem vniⁱ aſtri eleuaʈ ſufficies materia ꝓ cometa:igiʈ per virtutem pluriⁱ aſtroꝛ eleuaʈ ſufficiens materia ꝓ galatia.Lⁱ ſcðo qꞁ galacia non fiʈ inter tropicos:ꞇ hoc non eſt niſi qꞁ ibi eſt nimia caliditaⁱ:igitur ſigñ eſt cᷘ illo mð, fit galacia. Sed oppoſitum nunc tenetur:cum dicaͮ tur galacia eſſe circulus celeſtis qui parⁱ recipit de lumine.

Aristotle points to the stars in this illustration from a European edition of his writings, published in 1496. Aristotle believed that all things were composed of four elements: earth, water, air, or fire. Any one of these elements could be transformed by nature or by alchemy into any other.

downward. The "natural place" of water and earthy matter was at the center of the universe. Fire and air moved in the other direction, outward from the world. Aristotle's world, then, was the result of the inevitable falling together of all earthy matter, moving toward the center of the universe as its "natural place." The world was where it was simply because that was where the center of the universe was.

The stars had a different type of motion. Rather than going up or down, they were seen to travel in circles around the heavens. They never seemed to reach a "natural place" and stop. They carried on circling the sky. This, to Aristotle, suggested a different type of matter, a fifth element that he called "aether." The heavens had always been thought of as divine, and so the aether was given divine properties. It was perfect matter, unchanging and without blemish. The motion of the sphere of the stars was circular, perpetual, and frictionless.

The motion of the planets was observed to be circular too, but not perfectly so. They had strange, irregular orbits, and, to Aristotle, the planets were less divine than the stars.

Aristotle's universe was a ladder of increasing divinity, from the center of the Earth to the "sphere of the fixed stars" and beyond. But, to all practical purposes, it was two universes. The moon and beyond was one system—divine,

Scan here for a video that explains the Aristotelian-Ptolemaic cosmology:

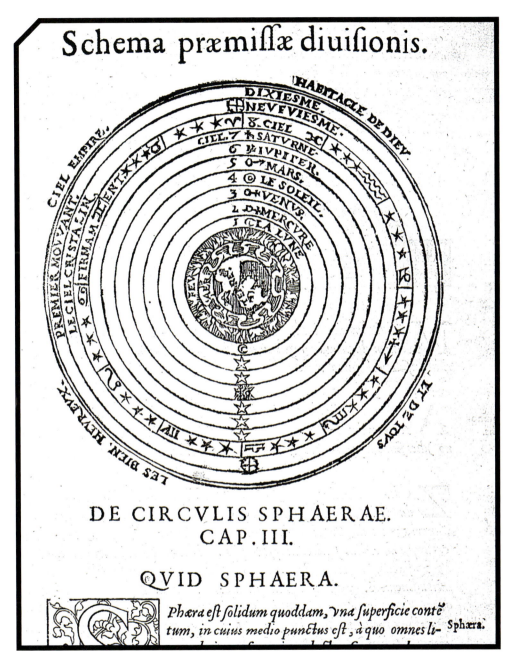

A corrupted view of Aristotle's universe mixed with Christian mythology in a European book published in 1551. The Earth is at the center; around it rotate the planets, the stars, and the nine orders of the angels, leading eventually to God.

unchanging, and perfect. But within the orbit of the moon was another: this was the realm of our world and the "four elements." Here, matter and motion obeyed very different laws.

Egyptian geographer and astronomer Claudius Ptolemy, who lived in the second century CE, modified Aristotle's view of the universe. His work was the culmination of the whole of ancient Greek astronomy. Although Ptolemy agreed generally with Aristotle's ideas, he tried to calculate the exact motion of the planets with mathematical precision. However, he still believed that the Earth was motionless at the center of the universe. The Aristotelian-Ptolemaic view was not seriously challenged until the sixteenth century.

The Sun-Centered Universe

Polish mathematician Nicolaus Copernicus was one of those who claimed that the sun was at the center, and not the Earth. It is true that in Ptolemy's calculations, the sun did seem to have a special relationship with each planet, but a **heliocentric** (sun-centered) universe was so much against common sense and theology that it was many years before Copernicus's friends persuaded him to publish his ideas. His historic book, *De Revolutionibus Orbium Coelestium* (*The Revolution of the Heavenly Orbs*), was printed in 1543, the year he died.

Mathematically, Copernicus's theory was perfect, but in terms of medieval physics, it certainly was not. His only successful justification of his work was in terms of simplicity, and it is true to say that his theory removed a whole layer of complexity from Ptolemy's mathematics. Even so, to avoid the book being banned by the Church, the publisher had to pass it off as a mathematical theory and nothing more.

Like most other astronomers, a Danish scholar named Tycho Brahe rejected Copernicus's work because it suggested that the Earth could move. Tycho thought the Earth "a hulking, lazy body unfit for motion," and developed a cosmology of his own. Although it appears very different from Copernicus's system, it is mathematically similar. But the Earth is at the center.

Tycho's work did bring advances. Temporary and variable phenomena like comets and **supernovas** (exploding stars) had always, since Aristotle, been

Statue of Polish astronomer Nicolaus Copernicus (1473–1543). His calculations convinced him that it was the sun, and not the Earth, that was at the center of the universe.

classified as meteorological events in the Earth's atmosphere. Such temporary events could never be regarded as part of the permanence and perfection of the heavens. But Tycho's careful observations of a supernova in 1572 put the "new star" at least as far away as Saturn. His calculation of the orbit of a comet in 1577 disproved the notion that there were hard, impenetrable spheres that guided the planets on their paths, for the comet seemed to pass right through them. In Tycho's cosmology, these hard spheres disappeared from the skies. The "perfection of the Heavens" was receiving its first dent.

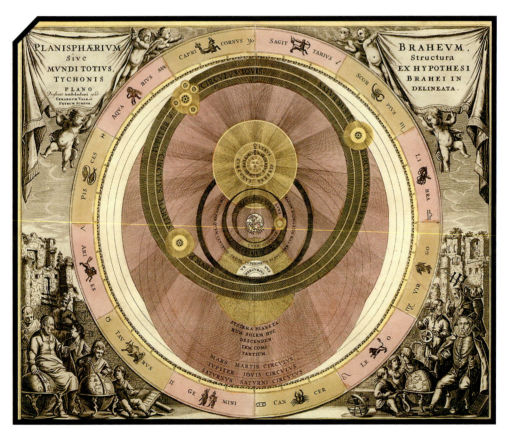

A drawing from 1716, showing the system of planetary movement proposed by Tycho Brahe. The Earth, at the center, stands still, while the sun and moon revolve around it. The other planets revolve around the sun. The illustration of Jupiter includes four moons discovered by Galileo in 1610. In the seventeenth century the Roman Catholic Church considered the Tychonic system to be a legitimate alternative to the system of Aristotle and Ptolemy, because the Earth was at the center.

TEXT-DEPENDENT QUESTIONS

1. Who provided the basic form of the geocentric model of the universe?
2. What were the five elements proposed by Aristotle?
3. What Egyptian astronomer modified Aristotle's view of the universe?

 RESEARCH PROJECT

To understand parallax, hold a pencil at arm's length. As you alternately open and close each eye, the pencil appears to move relative to the background. The closer you hold the pencil, the larger the movement of the pencil appears to be. If you know the distance between each eye and the angle of the apparent movement (the parallax angle), you can calculate how far away the pencil is.

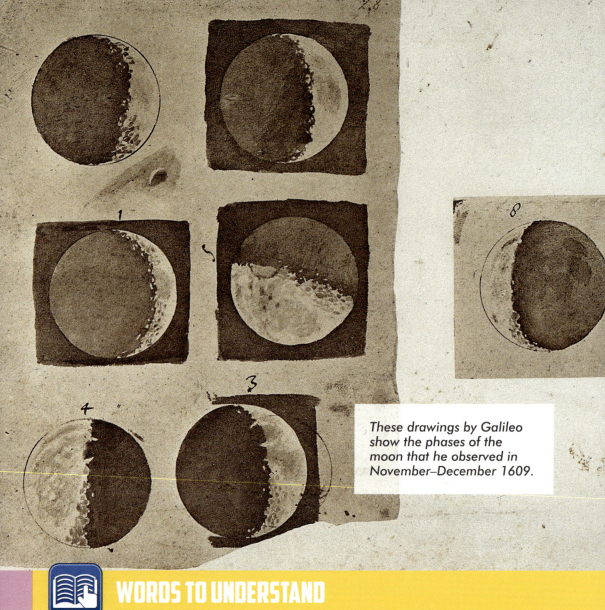

These drawings by Galileo show the phases of the moon that he observed in November–December 1609.

CHAPTER 3

The Telescope Discoveries

During the summer of 1609, Galileo's telescope was greatly admired in Venice. When the excitement finally died down, he had time to see what else the instrument had to offer. Naturally, he started looking up at the night sky.

When Galileo looked at the supposedly perfect sphere of the moon through his telescope, he saw a body covered with deep craters and high mountain ranges. Galileo could not imagine a more imperfect and less divine sphere. From the shadows that the mountains cast, he even estimated their height. He found the mountains to be about four miles (seven km) high—very similar to those on the "imperfect" Earth. The philosophers in the universities made hasty modifications to keep their philosophy untarnished.

One of the strongest arguments against the Copernican system was that the Earth was the only planet with a moon. (Before Galileo's time, the moon was considered another one of the planets that revolved around the Earth.) But to Galileo's surprise, when he looked at Jupiter through his telescope, he observed four moons circling the planet. Later, he noticed that Saturn, too, had "attendants," as he called them, although these seemed to behave rather curiously. It was not until 1655 that the more powerful telescopes of Dutch astronomer Christiaan Huygens were able to show that these "attendants" were not ordinary moons, but rings.

IN NOMINE DOMINI
NOSTRI IESV CHRISTI AMEN.

Enerale,& nouum Principium interpretationum Nobilissimæ, & Florentiss.me Academiæ Dominorum Philosophorum, & Medicorū Celeberrimi Patauini Gymnasii Anni præsentis 1593.Feliciter incipiet die III.Nouemb.sub Felicibus Auspiciis, Illustrissimorum D.D.Iustiniani Iustiniano ,pSereniss.,&Illust.Duc.Dom.Veneto Prętoris,& Nicolai Gussoni Præfecti Patauii,Magnificiquè,ac perillustris Domini Georgii Pipani Cracouiensis Poloni Rectoris digniss. Academiæ prædictæ , cum Lectionibus per horas distributis; Quas infrascripti admodum R.Magistri,et Exccellentiss. Domini Doctores,de mandato ipsius perillustris Domini Rectoris aggredientur,et prosequentur ordine,ut infra disposito,videlicet.

Ad Theologiam in via Sancti Thomæ.
Reuerendus Pater D.Magister. *Angelus Andronicus* } Leget Lib. primum sententiarum,hora tertia mane.

Ad Theologiam in via Scoti.
Reuerendus Pater D.Mag. Hieronymus Pallanterius a Castro Bononiensi. } Leget Epistolam D. Pauli ad Romanos diebus festiuis hora secunda mane.

Ad Lecturam Sacræ Scripturæ.
Reu.Pater D.Magister Alphonsus Sotus Florentinus.

Ad Metaphysicam in via Sancti Thomæ.
Reuerendus Pater D.Magister

Ad Metaphysicam in via Scoti.
Reuerendus Pater D.Magister Saluator Bartholutius de Assisio. } Leget lib. primum metaph.hora secunda mane.

Ad Theoricam ordinariam Medicinæ.
Excellentissimus D.Horatius Augenius Marchianus in primo loco. } Legent primam sen.Auicenæ hora prima.mane.
Excellentissimus.D. Albertinus Bottonus Patauinus in secundo loco.

Ad Practicam ordinariam Medicinæ.
Excellentissimus D.Alexander Massaria Vicetinus in primo loco. } Legent de Morbis particularibus a corde infra hora prima post meridiem.
Excellentissimus D.Hercules Saxonia Patauinus, in secundo loco.

Ad Philosophiam ordinariam.
Excellentissimus D.Franciscus Piccolomineus Senensis, in primo loco. } Legent primum, & secundum de Anima hora secunda post meridiem.
Excellentissimus D.Cæsar Cremoninus Centensis , in secundo loco.

Ad Theoricam extraordinariam Medicinæ.
Excellentissimus D.Anibal Bimbiolus in primo loco. } Legent artem paruam Galeni hora meridiei.
Excellentissimus D.Nicolaus Triuisinus Patauinus, in altero loco.

Ad Practicam extraord. Medicinæ.
Excellentissimus D.AEmilius Campilongius Patauinus in primo loco. } Legent de Morbis particularibus a capite usq; ad cor hora secunda mane.
Excellentissimus D.Alexander Vigontia Patauinus, in altero loco.

Ad Philosophiam extraordinariam.
Excellentissimus D.Camillus Bellonus Venetus in primo loco. } Legent tertium de Anima hora prima post merid.
Excellentissimus D.Schinella de Comitibus Patauinus, in altero loco.

Ad Philosophiam Moralem Aristotelis.
Locus uacat.

Ad Chirurgiam,et Anatomen.
Excellentissimus D. Hieronymus Fabricius de Aquapendente Etruscus. } Leget de ulceribus anatomen & fracturis hora 3.mane.

Ad Lecturam tertij libri Auicennæ.
Excellentissimus D: Antonius Niger Patauinus. } Leget de febribus hora secunda mane in diebus festiuis.

Ad Lecturam Simplicium.
Locus uacat in Gymnasio:sed in horto Mag.D. Iacobus Antonius Cortusius Patauinus , incipiet docere, die secunda Maii.1594.hora XXII.

Ad Logicam.
Excellentissimus D.Bernardinus Petrella Thuscus, in primo loco. } Legent lib. Secundum posteriorum hora prima mane.
Excellentissimus D.Faustinus Summus Patauinus,in secundo loco.

Excellentissimus D.Priamus Businellus Patauinus,in tertio loco. } Leget lib.Tert. post.in diebus festiuis. hora secunda.

Ad Mathematicam.
Excellentissimus D.Galileus de Galileis Florentinus. } Leget Sphæram & Euclidem, hora tertia post merid.

Ad Humanitatem Græcam, & Latinam.
Excellentissimus D.Antonius Riccobonus ciuis Rhodiginus,&Patauinus. } Retoricam Aristotelis & epigramatā Greca.

Laus Deo Optimo Maximo.

PATAVII, ex officio Almæ Vniuersitatis Artistarum præscripti Gymnasii.Die III. Nouembris. M.D.XCIII.
Marcus Antonius Coradinus Canc. Mand.

Patauii,apud Laurentium Pas. Typog. Vtriusq; Vniuersitatis.

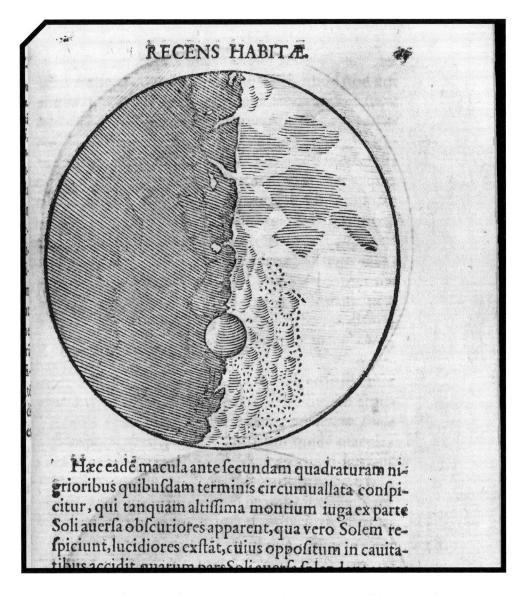

RECENS HABITÆ.

Hæc eadē macula ante secundam quadraturam nigrioribus quibusdam terminis circumuallata conspicitur, qui tanquam altissima montium iuga ex parte Soli auersa obscuriores apparent, qua vero Solem respiciunt, lucidiores exstat, cuius oppositum in cauitatibus accidit quarum pars Soli auersa

Opposite page: This 1593 list of lecturers at the University of Padua includes Galileo, who taught mathematics at the school from 1592 until 1610. That year, the success of Galileo's book about his telescopic observations, Sidereus Nuncius (The Starry Messenger), enabled him to leave the university and spend more time on his investigations.

Above: One of Galileo's drawings of the surface of the moon, reproduced in Sidereus Nuncius, shows it to be rough and pitted.

For a short video about Tycho Brahe, scan here:

The discovery of moons that orbited Jupiter meant that the Earth was not unique. And, what was more, if planets like Jupiter could be at the center of motion for their moons, then there was no reason the sun could not be the center of motion for the planets, as Copernicus's theory required.

Some philosophers refused to believe that their time-honored beliefs could be wrong. They claimed that a clever optical trick in Galileo's telescopes had made Jupiter's moons appear in the sky. Galileo offered a reward to anyone who could make a telescope that put moons around one planet but not around another. The reward was never claimed. Galileo wrote to Kepler, "What would you say of the learned here, who ... have steadfastly refused to cast a glance through the telescope? What shall we make of this? Shall we laugh, or shall we cry?"

The Ptolemaic cosmology had important differences from both the Tychonic and Copernican systems. According to Ptolemy, Venus passed by the sun on one side only, rather than revolving around it, for example. Before the development of the telescope, observers had not been able to see whether this was correct or not. But when Galileo looked through his telescope, he saw that Venus, like our moon, showed **phases** during which it was illuminated by the sun. When Galileo compared these phases with the position of Venus relative to the sun, he recognized that Venus did, in fact, orbit the sun as Copernicus had said.

The evidence was mounting. Galileo's discovery of the lunar mountains and his later observations of **sunspots** began to undermine the concept of the perfect heavens. His observations of Venus had disproved the Ptolemaic system, while no evidence had yet been found against the Copernican system.

But the telescope had not provided any firm evidence against Tycho's system. There were only two differences between this system and the Copernican cosmology. Each put a different body at the center of the universe, and, according to the Copernican system, the Earth moved. But the stars at the perimeter of the universe were too far away for anyone to calculate whether it was the sun or the Earth that was actually at the center.

Title page of the original edition of Sidereus Nuncius, *published in Venice in 1610.*

Galileo had to contest the Tychonic system on the grounds of the motion of the Earth. His as-yet unpublished work on the laws of motion and inertia would, he thought, take care of that.

This NASA photo shows three of Jupiter's moons (Europa at lower left, Callisto above it, and Io at upper right) passing in front of the giant planet. (The black marks are shadows cast by Europa and Callisto as they orbit.) These three moons, along with Ganymede, were observed by Galileo in January 1610. He called them the "Medicean stars," in hopes of currying favor with the powerful Medici family. Today, they are known as the Galilean moons, to distinguish them from the many other smaller bodies that orbit Jupiter. Modern astronomers have named fifty-three moons circling Jupiter, and have identified sixteen additional moons that have not yet been named.

In 1610, within a few months of his first discoveries, Galileo had rushed into print. His book *Sidereus Nuncius* (*The Starry Messenger*) made Galileo famous overnight. Astronomers all over Europe wanted to see these things for themselves. The demand for good telescopes, especially those from Galileo's own workshop, was impossible to satisfy. What made his telescopes important were their power and quality. Sometimes he ground the lenses himself. Whereas Lippershey's telescope magnified only three times, Galileo made instruments that magnified eight, twenty and, finally, thirty times. Two of these instruments are preserved today in Florence, Italy.

It was an exciting time for Galileo. In September 1610, he left Padua for Florence, and began to devote all his time to research. He became court mathematician and philosopher to Cosimo II de' Medici, the grand duke of Tuscany, who was a former pupil. He had named Jupiter's moons the "Medicean stars" in honor of the grand duke—an obvious hint, but it worked.

In 1611, Galileo took his telescopes with him on a triumphant tour of Rome. Everyone—including the astronomers at the Jesuit Theological College—was convinced that his discoveries were real. He was invited to become a member of the first truly "scientific" society in the world, a society in which university men were conspicuously absent. The Accademia dei Lincei (Academy of the Keen-Eyed) put more trust in observation and experiment than in philosophy or the works of authority.

In 1612, Galileo published his first book on pure physics, about the effects of **surface tension**. It was a masterpiece of the power of observation and experiment over the preconceptions of Aristotelian philosophers. Galileo became more confident about his ideas. The next year, in a heated exchange of letters with one of the Jesuit astronomers about the nature of sunspots, Galileo supported Copernicus openly for the first time. The Accademia dei Lincei published Galileo's writings as a short book titled *Letters on Sunspots* in 1613. In the book, Galileo implied that the truth of Copernicus's theory was so plain to see that there was nothing to fear in supporting it.

However, Galileo was very wrong in this belief. It was one thing for astronomers and theologians to confirm his discoveries, but quite another for them to agree

THE CATHOLIC CHURCH UNDER ATTACK

The Roman Catholic Church originated in the early days of Christianity, and claims to have been established by the Apostle Peter, one of Jesus's most important followers. For more than 1,000 years, most Christians who lived in the western Roman Empire—Europe and North Africa—respected and obeyed the authority of the Roman Catholic leader: the Pope. Church leaders were in charge of teaching how Christians should live. Books were rare and few people could read, so the Church could controlled what most people learned. The pope and other church leaders interpreted the scriptures, and also taught things that were not included in the Bible. These, Church leaders said, were the traditions and teachings of the apostles and the early Christians.

During the fifteenth and sixteenth centuries, some Christians in Europe began to grow concerned about certain practices that Roman Catholic leaders permitted. They began to protest against things like plenary indulgences, in which the church promised to forgive sins in exchange for financial donations. Beginning around 1517, people such as Martin Luther, a Roman Catholic monk from Germany, and Frenchman John Calvin led the opposition to these corrupt practices. When Church leaders did not change their ways, the reformers broke away from the Roman Catholic Church and established what became known as Protestant churches. The reform movement became known as the Protestant Reformation.

Religious disagreements between Protestants and Catholics led to wars throughout Europe. Some rulers remained faithful to the Catholic Church. Others supported the Lutherans or Calvinists. Between 1524 and 1648—a period that covers Galileo's entire lifetime—there was constant fighting among Catholics and Protestants throughout Europe.

Martin Luther (1483–1546) was a key figure in the Reformation that divided the Christian Church.

One of the major points of conflict was over how people understood the Bible. Luther and other reformers believed that everyone should read and understand the holy scriptures for themselves, rather than blindly trusting the Catholic Church's interpretation. The invention of the printing press a few decades earlier meant the Bible and other books could be made available to more people. Luther and other reformers soon published translations of the Bible into German, French, English, and other languages. Due to the long conflict, the Catholic Church came to view anyone who questioned its teachings as a potential threat.

Galileo was tutor of the teenaged Cosimo de' Medici (1590–1621) from 1605 to 1608. When Cosimo succeeded his father as Grand Duke of Tuscany in 1609, his patronage enabled Galileo to leave his position at the University of Padua and concentrate on scientific experiments and writings.

with a cosmology for which Galileo had found no firm proof. In supporting Copernicus, he had "contradicted a universal opinion held by all philosophers," warned a friend in Rome.

Galileo had indeed made enemies. A group had formed to oppose him, made up of his old enemies at Pisa, a few minor but noisy clergymen, and others who had been on the receiving end of his attacks. Some were envious of his new position with the grand duke. Others hated him for his growing disrespect for "true philosophy." They decided that his Copernican views were too important for academic argument. The anti-Galileo group succeeded in getting what Copernicus's work had avoided to that point—the attention of the Catholic Church in Rome.

In 1616, a committee of churchmen decreed that teaching that the Earth moved around the sun was theologically wrong. Future publication of Copernicus's book was suspended "for correction," and Galileo was told that he must not "hold, teach, or defend" the Copernican case again. It could only be used as a mathematical hypothesis, and nothing more.

Bitterly disappointed and angry, Galileo returned to Florence. His attack on the immobility of the Earth was finished. The book he wanted to write challenging the Tychonic system was now, he thought, impossible.

 ## TEXT-DEPENDENT QUESTIONS

1. What Dutch astronomer identified the "attendants" of Saturn as rings?
2. What book published in 1610 made Galileo famous?
3. What were the Medicean Planets?

 ## RESEARCH PROJECT

Using the internet or your school library as a guide, create a model of the "celestial spheres" proposed by Ptolemy. Include the ecliptic path—the route that the Sun follows through the sky from Earth's perspective.

Galileo was so confident in the truth of the Copernican system, and in his friendship with Pope Urban VIII that he failed to see how publishing a book that endorsed Copernicus's cosmology would threaten the Roman Catholic Church.

WORDS TO UNDERSTAND

contravene—to violate, or come into conflict with, a prohibition, order, or law.

elliptical orbit—the revolving of one object around another in an oval-shaped path called an ellipse. Most objects in space travel in elliptical orbits.

tortuous—not direct or straightforward.

CHAPTER 4

The Motion of the Earth

During the years that followed, Galileo kept silent about Copernican ideas. Even when he was engaged in an argument with Jesuit astronomers about the nature of comets, he did not mention Copernicus.

In 1623, a new pope was elected. He was Maffeo Barberini, a nobleman and diplomat from Florence. Galileo and Barberini had met more than a decade earlier, because Barberini was interested in experimental science. After Barberini was anointed Pope Urban VIII, Galileo traveled to Rome to congratulate him personally.

However, when Galileo approached Barberini about writing a book on the Copernican system, the pope was not so sure. The Roman Catholic Church was under great pressure due to the Protestant Reformation and religious warfare in Europe, and the pope was responsible for upholding the entirety of Christian belief. Eventually, the pope agreed to let Galileo write his book, but he provided some conditions. The work was to be a balanced discussion of the rival systems, and no conclusion was to be reached. In addition, Urban VIII asked Galileo to include some of his own arguments against the Copernican system in the text.

When Urban VIII agreed to let Galileo write his book, he was not aware of the 1616 decision by the Church committee that prohibited Galileo from teaching or defending Copernicus's theory. Galileo never mentioned the matter, which turned out to be a huge mistake.

An Influential Book

Dialogue Concerning the Two Chief World Systems: Ptolemaic and Copernican was published in 1632. The book was written in Italian (rather than in Latin, as was customary) so that any well-informed layman could read it. The first printing sold out within months.

Dialogue was written not as a dry, mathematical work, but presented as a lively argument between friends. These friends discussed the points for and against each system. Galileo used logical and commonsense arguments, the results of experiments and observation.

But *Dialogue* can hardly be said to present a balanced argument. Galileo clearly favored the Copernican system over the cosmologies proposed by Ptolemy (which few astronomers still believed) and Tycho Brahe (who, like Ptolemy, had placed the stationary Earth at the center of the universe.) If Copernicus was correct, both Ptolemy and Tycho must be wrong.

The arguments against the Copernican system—including those that Urban VIII had asked Galileo to include—boiled down to one problem: If the Earth moves, either on its own axis or around the sun, why are people not aware of that motion? Galileo's work on the laws of motion at Pisa and Padua had shown him how all these arguments could be answered logically.

Galileo had to argue against the Aristotelian thinkers, who had very deep philosophical misgivings about any motion of the Earth. He also had to convince them that their distinction between the physics of the heavens and of the Earth was no longer valid. Circular motion was, to Galileo, just as natural for the Earth as for the heavens. Against the Aristotelian preconceptions, his science of motion was a powerful weapon.

Galileo began, like Copernicus, by justifying the Earth's rotation in terms of simplicity. To expect the whole universe to rotate every day around a small, stationary Earth was unreasonable. It was rather like a person who expected the landscape to rotate about her, instead of bothering to turn her head.

There were strong arguments that the Earth moved around the sun over the course of a year. Galileo explained that what people on Earth see in the sky is the result

Maffeo Barberini (1568–1644) was elected Pope Urban VIII in August 1623. During his time as pope, Europe was suffering through the deadliest religious war in its history, the Thirty Years' War of 1618 to 1648. Because of the threat this conflict posed to the Roman Catholic Church's authority in Europe, the pope could not permit challenges to the Church's teachings.

DIALOGO
DI
GALILEO GALILEI LINCEO
MATEMATICO SOPRAORDINARIO
DELLO STVDIO DI PISA.

E Filosofo, e Matematico primario del

SERENISSIMO

GR. DVCA DI TOSCANA.

Doue ne i congreßi di quattro giornate si discorre
sopra i due

MASSIMI SISTEMI DEL MONDO
TOLEMAICO, E COPERNICANO;

*Proponendo indeterminatamente le ragioni Filosofiche, e Naturali
tanto per l'vna, quanto per l'altra parte.*

CON PRI   VILEGI.

.IN FIORENZA, Per Gio: Batista Landini MDCXXXII.

CON LICENZA DE' SVPERIORI.

of two different motions: They view the simple orbits of the planets around the sun from a position (the Earth) that is itself moving. This explained some of the awkward irregularity of the planets' motions.

Inertia and Movement

Galileo than attacked age-old arguments against the Earth's motion. This is the most important part of the whole book. One of the concepts he used was inertia. Galileo wrote that if a hard, smooth sphere is placed on a hard, smooth, horizontal surface and pushed gently, there is no reason for it to either speed up or slow down. Its motion in a straight line will be "conserved" and, in such an ideal situation, the sphere will continue rolling at the same speed forever. In this theoretical idea, the sphere can only change speed if another force is applied. The concept of inertia, although simple, was a great step forward in the history of science.

One of the greatest arguments against a rotating Earth was that falling weights fall straight down. The reasoning was this: An object that was allowed to fall freely—say, from a tower—always fell straight down, toward the center of the Earth. If the Earth *did* rotate, then wouldn't the spot on the ground that was under the object when it started to fall have moved, so the object would land in an entirely different place? The Aristotelian thinkers claimed that to someone standing on a moving Earth, the object seem to fall at an angle, not straight down. To prove this, an experiment was proposed: A weight would be dropped from the top of the mast on a ship that was sailing evenly and steadily around the world. The Aristotelians claimed that the weight would land toward the stern of the ship, rather than striking the deck beneath the mast.

But no one had every actually tried that experiment, and in *Dialogue* Galileo showed the fallacy in that reasoning. He drew a parallel between the sphere

Opposite page: The first page of Galileo's Dialogue Concerning the Two Chief World Systems, *published in 1632.*

on the horizontal surface and the weight dropped from the top of the ship's mast. Before being dropped, the weight obviously shared the same forward motion as the ship. When allowed to fall, there was no reason for the weight to lose this "indelibly impressed" forward motion, as Galileo called it. If the ship continued moving steadily, the weight would not overtake the deck below it, or be overtaken by it. The weight would fall at the foot of the mast. He applied the argument to the object dropped from the tower. To him, it was clear that the weight would fall vertically, whether the Earth was moving or not.

"We never see anything but the simple downward motion," wrote Galileo. "The other motion, common to the Earth, the tower and ourselves, remains imperceptible and as if non-existent."

The Spinning Earth Problem

If the Earth rotated, some doubters questioned how anything could stay on the Earth and not be thrown off into space. Galileo himself asked, "What weight, what tenacity of lime or mortar would hold rocks, buildings and whole cities so that they would not be hurled into the sky by such precipitous whirling?" The "precipitous whirling" that Galileo referred to was the rotation of the Earth every twenty-four hours.

Galileo used his discoveries about inertia to unravel the problem. Because he did not have a true understanding of centrifugal force, his argument was a **tortuous** one. A weight being whirled on a string did not fly directly outward when it was released, but continued to travel in a straight line from the point at which it was set free. In the same way, objects traveling on the surface of a rotating Earth would try to fly off the globe at a tangent and not at right angles to the surface. By staying on the Earth, we travel along a different path. Galileo wondered what difference there was between these two paths (tangential and circular) in, say, one second. That is, how far did an object "fall" by staying on the Earth rather than leaving it at a tangent? If this was greater than the distance that an object could free fall from rest, then the object would fly off.

As the Earth rotates, any point on its surface moves nearly one-third of a mile every second. Galileo worked out that, in that distance, a tangent to the Earth

Statues of Tycho Brahe and Johannes Kepler in Prague. Kepler's long study of the orbit of Mars led to his discovery of the elliptical paths of all the planets.

and the surface of the Earth itself were only separated by about 2 inches (5 cm). Gravity could cope with a "fall" of that distance in each second without difficulty, and so objects remained on the Earth.

To strict Aristotelians, this constant circular motion of all objects, as they rotated with the world, was, of course, impossible. According to the philosophy of Aristotle and Ptolemy, circular motion was not a "natural motion" of "earthy matter"—it belonged only to the heavens. But what, asked Galileo, was unnatural about circular motion? It was, after all, a combination of natural straight-line inertia and a "natural motion" toward the center. Once those facts were accepted, there was no barrier to considering the rotation of the Earth as natural, also.

Galileo never extended this idea to the motions of the planets around the sun. These orbits were not simple circles (Kepler had shown, in 1609, that they were **elliptical**), and Galileo's idea of "natural circular motion" could not explain them.

The Earth's motion around the sun could not, said Galileo, be proved by any Earth-based experiment. The situation was similar to being enclosed inside a windowless cabin on a moving ship in calm waters. No experiment could be made inside the cabin to prove that the ship was moving. A weight would still fall vertically. A bird would fly around the cabin, just as it would outside. What Galileo meant was that the physics in one steadily moving system (like the cabin of the ship) were indistinguishable from the physics of another (like those on dry land). This idea would become an essential principle of Isaac Newton's "classical" mechanics, as well as of Albert Einstein's theory of special relativity.

Despite this, however, Galileo thought he *had* found proof of the Earth's movement. He believed that the ocean tides showed that the Earth's motion was not quite steady. This unsteadiness was caused, he believed, by an interaction of its rotation about its own axis and its yearly motion around the sun. On one side of the Earth these two motions added together, on the other side they canceled. This "unevenness" caused a small movement of the seas, like the slopping around of water in a bowl when it is moved. (Galileo's argument, as it turned out, was not accurate either.)

Critical Reaction

The reaction to Galileo's *Dialogue* came swiftly and decisively. But this time, the trouble did not come from university philosophers. Galileo had made some enemies at the Jesuit College in Rome after becoming involved in some bitter personal disputes about the nature of sunspots and comets. The astronomers there informed the Church that they thought *Dialogue* was very one-sided. They said that Galileo had gone far beyond the conditions laid down by Barberini when he became pope ten years earlier. However, the Roman Catholic Church's official censor had reviewed and approved *Dialogue* in 1629, before it was published.

Rumors soon began circulating about what Galileo had actually been told he could or could not write. The Vatican records were searched for references to the events of 1616. When a record was found, it did not match what Galileo had been told. The report in the Vatican files was much more strongly worded. Under the conditions of the Vatican record, Galileo could not possibly have dared to approach Barberini about writing the book.

That record turned out to be a not-entirely-accurate account of what had happened in 1616. It was, perhaps, even a forgery. The respected cardinal who

To see a short video on the trial of Galileo, scan here:

Galileo's trial before the Holy Inquisition, 1633.

had handled the 1616 affair was dead. Galileo could not find his own copy of the instructions he had been given in 1616, but he did have a letter from the cardinal that supported his position.

Unfortunately for Galileo, the pope was notified about the matter before the problems with the Vatican record were recognized. Urban VIII flew into a rage. He was convinced that Galileo had fooled him and, worse still, lied to him. Galileo had not told the pope about the previous order from the Church concerning his Copernican views: neither his own version of the story, nor the version found in the Vatican's files. The pope thought Galileo had taken advantage of his good nature in order to get permission to write the book. The case was passed to the Holy Inquisition, and in October 1632 Galileo was summoned to Rome for trial.

This was beyond his worst fears. Illness and depression delayed the long winter journey south. But by February 1633, Galileo was on his way to Rome.

He was initially charged with **contravening** the Church's instructions to him back in 1616. But when it was clear that there was something wrong with the Vatican's records, the Holy Inquisition abandoned this charge. However, the Inquisition was not an impartial court of law. Its main purpose was to punish heretics and uphold true Christian doctrine.

Galileo could not be allowed to go free. The Copernican issue had been brought back into the open by publication of Galileo's *Dialogue*, and the Church had previously decided, in 1616, that those ideas were false and heretical. Furthermore, Galileo had not told the pope the entire truth before publishing the *Dialogue*. Consequently, Urban VIII insisted that Galileo be punished as an warning to others.

Because of this, Galileo recognized that the affair would inevitably conclude with his guilt, whatever the evidence showed. So, on the promise of leniency, he agreed to confess to wrongdoing. In a public statement, Galileo said that after rereading the book, he recognized that his own "vain ambitions and ignorance" had caused him to overstate the Copernican case. However, he added, "I do not hold and have not held this opinion of Copernicus since the command was given to me [in 1616] that I must abandon it. For the rest I am here in your hands—do with me as you please."

Everyone knew that this was not the truth, but as a confession, it was enough. Galileo had little alternative but to deny the Copernican "falsehood." The threat of torture by the Inquisition was real, and all prisoners were formally shown the instruments of torture as a reminder before going to trial. Just three decades earlier, in 1600, an Italian cleric named Giordano Bruno who had written

Galileo kneels before a Bible as he recants his beliefs to the Holy Inquisition. By the end of his 1633 trial, Galileo was a tired and broken man.

books disagreeing with Church doctrine about astronomy was convicted by the Inquisition and was burned at the stake.

Galileo was sentenced on June 22, 1633. He was to serve life imprisonment. Publication of *Dialogue Concerning the Two Chief World Systems* was banned, and remained so for nearly 200 years. And Galileo was forbidden to write any further books.

Galileo was staggered. He had believed that he would be treated leniently, as he had been promised. However, the conditions of his imprisonment were soon relaxed. He was allowed to leave Rome to spend his exile at the home of the archbishop of Siena, whom he knew well. After only five months there, Galileo was allowed back to his own villa at Arcetri, in the hills outside Florence. However, he was still kept under house arrest.

TEXT-DEPENDENT QUESTIONS

1. What were the conditions Pope Urban VII asked Galileo to observe if he wrote a book about the Copernican system?

2. What simple concept did Galileo use to attack arguments against the Earth's motion?

3. What was the purpose of the Holy Inquisition's trial of Galileo?

4. What was Galileo's punishment when he confessed to wrongdoing?

RESEARCH PROJECT

Beginning in the twelfth century, the Christian Church implemented a new program throughout Europe. The purpose of the Holy Inquisition was to identify those who held beliefs that Church leaders thought posed a threat to their religious teachings. Those arrested by the Inquisition were often tortured until they admitted to crimes. Using your school library or the internet, find out more about the work of the Inquisition. Write a two-page report and share it with your class.

The interior of the villa where Galileo lived while under house arrest. He was well treated after his trial, and was even allowed a servant to attend to him. A portrait of Galileo hangs over the desk.

WORDS TO UNDERSTAND

dynamics—a branch of mechanics dealing with what happens to matter when under the action of forces, and when movement results.

parabola—a curve formed by cutting a cone parallel to one of its sloping sides.

statics—a branch of mechanics dealing with the behavior of matter under the action of forces, when the system is in equilibrium and no motion is taking place.

CHAPTER 5

Mechanics and Motion

Galileo's work on astronomy was firmly and irretrievably behind him. However, once he had recovered from the shock and despair of the trial, he was persuaded to put the finishing touches to his life's work on **statics** and **dynamics**. Although he had been prohibited from publishing anything new, he secretly gave the manuscript to a Dutch friend, who published it in Leiden in 1638. (The Dutch Republic leaned toward the Protestant side in the religious wars of Europe, so the Church had not able to suppress the publication.) Galileo's book was called *Discourses and Mathematical Demonstrations Concerning Two New Sciences, Pertaining to Mechanics and Local Motion*. It was his final book, but scientifically it was his most important.

The new sciences concerned the "resistance of solid bodies to fracture" and the study of motion. The first of these sounds curious. It involved the breaking strength of solid beams in different situations, and grew out of Galileo's work on mechanics and his concept of the theory of matter.

Galileo was convinced that all matter was made up of particles. But what held the particles together? He thought it was due mostly to the effect of a vacuum between them. Like two smooth, flat plates held together, the particles resisted being pulled apart because of the "aversion of nature to empty space."

Galileo had noticed that a pump could never suck up water in a pipe to a height of more than about 34 feet (10.5 meters). He thought—incorrectly, as it turned out—that the column of water "broke" in the pipe when the force pulling the particles apart became too strong. (One of Galileo's associates,

Evangelista Torricelli, would eventually conduct studies to determine the physical properties of air, including pressure and resistance.)

When confronted with problems concerning, for instance, the way solid beams behaved under various loads, Galileo always reduced them to the principle of the lever or the balance. These were the "machines" of his mechanics. Although previous scientists had worked out all the basic ideas, no one had written so clearly about the foundations of mechanics as Galileo did. His early unpublished textbook on basic mechanics, *Il Mecchaniche*, was immensely useful to his students, and it was copied many times in Italy and abroad.

His predecessors had always treated statics and motion as entirely separate. To Galileo, however, the two were linked. A machine at rest was only a special case of a machine in motion. For instance, a balanced scale needs only the smallest weight to be added to one pan for it to start moving. Following are two of the areas in which Galileo's work on mechanics and motion was especially important.

Free Fall

In Galileo's early days, Aristotle dominated ideas on motion and change. The whole of nature was, to Aristotle, an interplay of rest and motion. To study the basis of motion was to study the basis of nature. Aristotle looked for the reasons behind motion—why it occurred. But exactly how objects moved received less attention.

Scholars in sixteenth-century Italy had produced quite a number of ideas about motion and free fall, but few results. For instance, it had not been determined whether, if air resistance was ignored, a heavy body accelerated continually from rest or whether it soon acquired a constant velocity.

In *Two New Sciences*, Galileo proved all his laws of free fall in his favorite and most rigorous way: by using pure mathematics. Through his experiments, Galileo determined that all bodies accelerate at the same rate, regardless of their size or mass. He showed that there is a relationship between the speed at which an object falls, the time it is falling, and the distance it covers while falling. Galileo found that falling bodies start very slowly but accelerate steadily. He determined

Title page of Galileo's 1638 book Discourses and Mathematical Demonstrations Concerning Two New Sciences, Pertaining to Mechanics and Local Motion, *published in Leiden in 1638.*

An illustration from an English edition of Galileo's Two New Sciences, *showing how the strength of a loaded beam is affected by its thickness and its length.*

that the distance (*d*) that a falling object travels increases in proportion (*a*) to the time (*t*) that it is falling, as described in the formula *dat²*.

Galileo also proposed that objects always have a velocity. However, sometimes that velocity has a magnitude of zero—which means the object is at rest. According to Galileo, a force is required to put an object into motion. Objects resist change in motion—a principle that came to be called "inertia."

Apart from Galileo's rather general concept of inertia, these laws were probably the most important statements he made. The way he discovered the relationship between velocity, distance, and time was, however, far from simple. It required several years of painstaking experiment, observation, and mathematical study.

To study motion in detail, Galileo needed to slow down the whole procedure. He did this by rolling an object—usually a small, smooth sphere—down a tilted surface, or inclined plane. In this way, the motion was slower than ordinary free fall and could more easily be measured. He proved that the speed of the ball at the bottom of the surface was just the same as if it had fallen the same vertical distance in free fall. No clocks measuring seconds were available, so he often used his pulse beat to measure the time in his experiments. Sometimes he used a water clock. This was basically a bucket of water with a small hole pierced in the bottom so that it leaked at a constant rate. By opening and closing the hole with a finger, time intervals could be estimated by measuring the amount of water that had leaked out. Galileo repeated his experiments many times so that he would get an accurate average. By measuring how far a sphere fell down an inclined plane in successive beats, the dat^2 relationship was discovered.

This was simple enough. What was harder to measure experimentally was velocity. In a letter written to a friend in 1604, Galileo connected the increase in velocity that occurred in free fall with the distance that the object dropped, not the time. This is wrong, but he was not alone in thinking this way. Almost every investigator before him had thought the same. Guided by Aristotle's idea that a body accelerated as it got nearer to its "natural place," they tended to relate

Galileo noting his observations while under house arrest.

velocity in proportion to distance fallen (v∝d). It was only when Galileo checked his mathematics some years later that he realized something was wrong. By 1609, he had worked out that the velocity was proportional to the time, not the distance—a formula he expressed as *v∝t*.

Galileo's third law of motion related all three quantities; velocity, time, and distance fallen. In his book he proved it very simply using an idea that had been used in the Middle Ages in Oxford, England. He plotted velocity (v) against time (t) in the same way as a modern graph is drawn. The distance traveled at any time is equivalent to the area under the graph (½vt). By showing motion in this graphical way (½vt = d), Galileo cut out many problems, since the motion was defined at every point. It is a good example of applying mathematics to solving physical problems.

Galileo's ideas about such concepts as momentum, power, and force were not well defined and were sometimes ambiguous. He often used different words to say the same thing. He never distinguished between mass and the effect of gravity on that mass, which is weight. Science would have to wait for Isaac Newton to make more exact distinctions.

Inertia and Projectiles

Of all types of motion, the behavior of projectiles received the most attention in Galileo's time. It was particularly important for gunnery and warfare. But this was also a complicated type of motion. Without an understanding of the laws of free fall, it is not surprising that no one before Galileo could accurately predict the flight of an object.

To Aristotle, any motion, like that of a projectile, that was not entirely free fall (or "natural") was in some way "forced." "Forced" motion took the moving object away from its "natural place," just as a "natural" motion took it toward its "natural place." All motion could be described in terms of one or both of these two opposite motions. But Aristotle began to go wrong when he tried to analyze these two types of motion.

The stage seemed set for the entry of the principle of inertia, "the first article in the creed of science," as it has been called. But, like the Copernican universe, physics had not developed enough for inertia to be the next step. A different idea emerged among the Aristotelian thinkers. At first glance, it appears similar, and it does describe what people observed.

According to this theory, when a cannon was fired, a certain amount of "impressed force" or "impetus" was transmitted to the cannonball by the explosion of the powder. But this was not the "indelibly impressed force," or inertia, that Galileo would later describe in *Two New Sciences*. It was only a temporary effect. This impetus was thought to diminish with time and fade away, just like heat, or the sound of a bell. Thus, a cannonball that was shot upward could not continue upward forever. According to this theory, at the top of the cannonball's flight, the impetus had died away, and the cannonball started to free fall as its "natural" motion took over. To medieval thinkers, the temporary nature of "forced" motion was obvious—nothing "forced" could carry on forever.

This was a far cry from the principle of inertia discussed earlier. Why did the impetus "leak away"? Air resistance was one reason. Another possibility was that the projectile was being forced upward against its natural inclination. This was thought to cause conflict and friction within the projectile and the impetus was weakened.

Scan here to see a short video on Galileo's experiments on motion and inertia:

At Pisa and Padua, Galileo started devising very simple experiments on motion, using spheres, surfaces, and pendulums. The results of those experiments revolutionized his thinking and took him far away from the Aristotelian preconceptions of his colleagues. He began to wonder about the movement of a perfect sphere on a flat, horizontal plane. To Galileo, this motion was neither "natural" nor "forced." He called it "neutral" motion. We now call this type of motion "inertia," and it is fundamental to a correct theory of projectile motion.

Inertia was very difficult to show experimentally, because no surface or sphere could be made smooth enough. Galileo decided on a different approach. He wanted to see whether inertia continued in mid-air. This would avoid the friction of the sphere against the surface.

He rolled a ball down inclined planes of different lengths. He then deflected the ball a short way along a tabletop. In this way, the ball rolled horizontally with certain different velocities. At the edge of the table, the ball rolled off and fell to

Understanding motion, force, and velocity was very important to the rulers of Renaissance Europe, as these laws could be utilized to improve weapons.

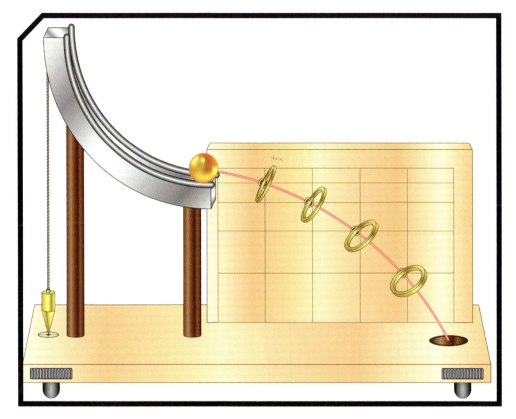

Galileo devised experiments like this to measure the velocity of a horizontal projectile.

the ground. For each velocity, Galileo noted where it hit the ground. The results were as he expected. The horizontal speed of the ball was maintained in the air before it hit the ground—the faster the ball was moving when it left the tabletop, the further it flew.

Another important point resulted from this experiment. In the results recorded within his manuscript, Galileo marked the trajectories of the ball after it left the table. They are quite clearly **parabolic**. His knowledge of geometry gave him the proof he needed. With constant motion horizontally, he knew that the vertical drop had to be dat^2 to fit the curve. But this was exactly the rule for free fall that he knew already. He had found that the path of a projectile was parabolic. He

After his trial, Galileo continued his experiments while under house arrest. From 1633 until 1642, he lived at the Villa Il Gioiello in the hills outside of Florence.

had also solved another problem that had troubled scholars. His work confirmed that the two components of motion, the vertical free fall and the horizontal inertial constant speed, were independent of each other. They did not interfere— "natural" and "forced" motion could be mixed.

Toward a Theory of Gravity

For convenience, Galileo used the words "natural" and "forced" all his life, but the great Aristotelian distinction between the two had been removed. Galileo's work shows the beginning of the understanding of Isaac Newton's concept of gravity, as well as the idea that the cause of any motion is merely the effect of different forces. But the nature of these forces was a mystery to Galileo. He wrote, "We do not really understand what principle or force it is that moves stones downward, any more than we understand what moves them upward after they leave the thrower's hand, or what moves the moon around."

Like Copernicus, Galileo was convinced that the sun, moon, and planets were kept in one piece by the same "gravity" that held the Earth together. But he was far away from making the next jump—wondering whether that same "gravity" kept the planets and moons in their orbits. Galileo had greatly admired the experimental work of William Gilbert, who had demonstrated around 1600 that the Earth behaved like a large magnet. Galileo thought, as did Kepler in Germany at the same time, that the planets may well be held in their orbits "as if by some magnetic attraction." It was not until 1687 that Newton was able to offer a more accurate explanation in the form of his "Law of Universal Gravitation."

 TEXT-DEPENDENT QUESTIONS

1. What was the subject of Galileo's book that was published in 1638?
2. How did Galileo prove the laws of free fall?
3. How did Galileo test whether inertia could continue in mid-air?

 RESEARCH PROJECT

Using the internet or your school library, find out more about astronomer Johannes Kepler and his laws of planetary motion. Write a two-page report and share it with your class.

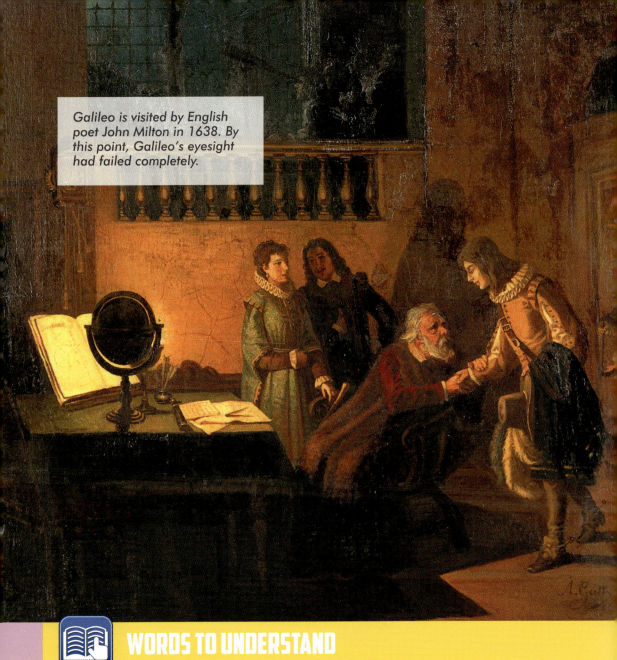

Galileo is visited by English poet John Milton in 1638. By this point, Galileo's eyesight had failed completely.

WORDS TO UNDERSTAND

convent—a Christian community in which women, known as nuns, devote themselves to religious life.

disciple—a follower or student of a teacher or leader.

rheumatism—a disease marked by inflammation and pain in the joints or muscles, such as arthritis.

CHAPTER 6

Galileo's Final Years

Even during the last few years of his long life, Galileo stayed remarkably active. Apart from finishing *Two New Sciences*, he continued his work on motion and on percussion. He began writing a new book on Euclid's mathematics only a few months before he died. At Arcetri, he was allowed to write and receive letters. He was even allowed some important visitors, such as poet John Milton from England. He found time for more relaxation too. He was often in his garden tending the vines that were his pride and joy. It was a great sadness for him when illness eventually forced him to stop drinking wine, which he adored. He used to call it "light held together by moisture."

Galileo never married but, in the early 1600s, he had three children by a Florentine woman named Marina Gamba. They had parted amicably in 1610, and his two daughters entered a **convent**. He became especially close to the eldest, Virginia, and he had moved to the villa at Arcetri to be nearer to her. She was a great comfort to him after his first trial in 1616 and after the death of his mother in 1620. When Virginia died in 1634, it was a great tragedy for him. For months he lost interest in everything.

In early 1637, Galileo began to have trouble with his eyesight, and by August he was totally blind. He was unable to read his *Two New Sciences* when the book was published a year later.

Galileo's only son, Vincenzio, joined his father for the last year or so of his life. Together they talked of plans to build a pendulum clock. The idea was

This portrait of a nun is traditionally identified as Sister Maria Celeste, daughter of Galileo Galilei.

based on Galileo's observations of the swinging chandelier in Pisa Cathedral over fifty years earlier. He dictated a design, and Vincenzio later began to make a working model. But it was never completed. The credit for the first practical pendulum clock went instead to Dutch scientist Christiaan Huygens, who started making his first model in 1656, entirely independently of the Galileis.

One of Galileo's keenest pupils, Vincenzio Viviani, joined him in 1639 and stayed with him until his death, writing letters for him and acting as his assistant. He later wrote a biography of his master. During the final months of Galileo's life, they were visited by another former pupil, Evangelista Torricelli, who had become a respected mathematician and scientist.

When he was about forty years old, Galileo had caught a severe cold that nearly killed him. Throughout the rest of his life he was troubled by attacks of **rheumatism** and other illnesses. During his final years, the attacks became worse and more frequent. In November 1641 he was confined to bed with fever and a kidney complaint, and on January 9, 1642, he died.

Galileo was allowed only a simple tomb in the Church of Santa Croce in Florence, and it was nearly 100 years before the authorities would allow a more

Scan here to see a modern version of the pendulum clock designed by Galileo:

71

GALILAEVS GALILEIVS PATRIC. FLOR.
GEOMETRIAE ASTRONOMIAE PHILOSOPHIAE MAXIMVS RESTITVTOR
NVLLI AETATIS SVAE COMPARANDVS
HIC BENE QVIESCAT
VIX.A.LXXVIII.OBIIT.A.CIƆ.IƆ.C.XXXXI.
CVRANTIBVS AETERNVM PATRIAE DECVS
X.VIRIS PATRICIIS SACRAE HVIVS AEDIS PRAEFECTIS
MONIMENTVM A VINCENTIO VIVIANO MAGISTRI CINERI SIBIQVE SIMVL
TESTAMENTO E I.
HERES IO. BAPT. CLEMENS NELLIVS IO. BAPT. SENATORIS F.
LVBENTI ANIMO ABSOLVIT.
AN. CIƆ.IƆ.CCXXXVII.

The tomb of Galileo is located inside the Basilica di Santa Croce in Florence, Italy.

impressive tomb to be built for him. Italy's "Man of Science" is now buried close to Italy's "Man of Art," Michelangelo.

Galileo's Scientific Legacy

The success of modern science began with the rise in importance of experiment and mathematics. That movement began before Galileo was born and is still continuing, but his part was an important and fundamental one. How did experimenting and mathematics fit into his method?

Watching his father's musical experiments gave Galileo an idea of the value of practical testing at an early age. But, surprisingly, he hardly mentions his investigations at all in his books. Most of what we know has been found in his day-to-day notebooks, or learned from stories about his life. This is very different from later scientists—men like chemist Robert Boyle, who reported their experiments in great detail. Galileo's experiments were, it seems, for his own purposes only. He liked to test for himself whether a particular idea was right. Once he had convinced himself, he used whatever means he saw fit to convince everyone else. Sometimes he used commonsense arguments but, wherever possible, the proof was a mathematical one.

But the followers of Aristotle denied that mathematics could describe anything else but the basic form of objects. Geometry could describe a wooden ball as a sphere, but it could say nothing about important properties such as its color or material. Mathematics, they said, could only be used divorced from the object itself. Galileo did not agree. His training was in mathematics and his love was mathematics. As a student, he had admired the way Archimedes had applied mathematics to the problems of mechanics. "The book of the universe," wrote Galileo, "is written in the language of mathematics, and its characters are triangles, circles, and other geometric figures without which it is humanly impossible to understand a single word of it." There were complications to this approach, such as friction and irregularities of surface, but an underlying basis of mathematics could be produced, and Galileo attempted to show this.

Galileo tried to reduce all problems to basic quantities like weight, distance, time, and speed. These were quantities that mathematics could deal with. Aristotle's four elements had no place in this system—Galileo's experiments showed that the laws of mechanics did not depend upon them. The weight of a body was all that seemed to matter. Seventeenth-century science soon ceased to be concerned with earth, water, air, and fire, and other theories of matter replaced them.

But what of the other philosophers? The Aristotelian university men were not really true to their master at all. Aristotle had never carried out experiments as such, but he had been a great observer as well as a philosopher. He had said that the process of uncovering the all-important causes underlying any change had to be a step-by-step process "from what is known to what is not known." Once these causes were found, they could then be used as a basis for explaining other related changes. But the Aristotelians of the Middle Ages concerned themselves with only one side of this scheme. Convinced that Aristotle's causes were correct, they used them to explain everything. They rarely went back to the "real world" for evidence that might confirm or disprove those ideas. Most of these men could never have extended their knowledge beyond that of Aristotle.

Galileo's "experimental method" was open-ended. There was no limit to the use

CHURCH FORGIVENESS

It took hundreds of years, but authorities in the Roman Catholic Church eventually admitted that its condemnation of Galileo's views in 1633 had been wrong. In 1741 Pope Benedict XIV permitted the publication of a complete edition of Galileo's writings, including an edited version of *Dialogue Concerning the Two Chief World Systems*. In 1835, the Church removed the unedited *Dialogue* from its list of banned books. In October 1992, more than 350 years after Galileo's trial, Pope John Paul II officially declared that the Holy Inquisition had acted in good faith when it condemned Galileo, but that the scientist had been correct.

of practical testing or mathematics, so long as the rules governing each were followed. Once some simple principles had been laid down, more complex situations could be analyzed. From inertia and the laws of free fall, the parabolic paths of projectiles could be proved, as we have seen. As he wrote in his *Two New Sciences*, "My work is merely the beginning."

Indeed it was! Even before Galileo died, his work was being carried on by a small group of pupils and **disciples**. They used and extended his methods of experimentation and mathematics. One of them, Benedetto Castelli, developed another "new science"—that of the mechanics of flowing water, or hydrodynamics. Another, Bonaventura Cavalieri, carried out important work in mathematics. He worked particularly with problems in which a quantity, such as speed or distance, changed from one moment to the next (this was something that had concerned Galileo in his study of free fall). Perhaps Galileo's most famous pupil was Evangelista Torricelli. He too carried on Galileo's work, but his greatest achievement was the invention and explanation of the barometer.

Galileo's student Torricelli discovers the principle of the mercury barometer while experimenting in the Alps, 1643.

Galileo had been very much an Italian scientist. He rarely wrote to anyone outside Italy. Exasperated by the stubbornness of the Latin-speaking Aristotelian scholars, he wrote all his later books in Italian, so that any well-informed layman could read them. But this limited his immediate influence outside his own country, since few foreign scholars spoke the language. Latin translations of some of his books were made too late for them to have any great effect.

Even so, Galileo's influence was immense. His *Starry Messenger* had been written in Latin, and it made his name famous all over Europe. His textbook on mechanics, *Il Mecchaniche*, was often studied. And it was not long before a Latin translation of his *Two Chief World Systems* appeared in Europe. It became notorious all over Christendom. After Galileo's trial, all Roman Catholic astronomers were, officially, believers in the Tychonic system. But it was Galileo's book that, above all else, caused the tide of opinion to turn instead toward the system proposed by Copernicus.

International Fame

With the death of Galileo, most of the force left Italian science. But the real revolt against the "ancients" had already begun in other countries, especially France and England.

In France, Galileo's work was circulated by Marin Mersenne, who found his methods "a true programme for natural science." Philosopher and mathematician Rene Descartes was, however, less impressed. Descartes, like Galileo, believed that practical testing and mathematics were important, but he was, above all, a "rationalist." He was convinced of the importance of human reasoning. Whereas Galileo had used experimentation and mathematics to safeguard against errors of reasoning, Descartes worked the other way around. In his view, human reasoning provided the guide to what was right. Although his own reasoning tended to lead him to many wrong conclusions, it was a powerful method, and it dominated the work of many scientists throughout the seventeenth century.

Galileo's greatest influence was probably in England. In about 1645, a number of "natural philosophers" began to meet regularly at Gresham College in London. This group, which later developed into the Royal Society, discussed the "new or

French philosopher and mathematician René Descartes was the first person to formulate a clear definition of the concept of inertia.

Sir Isaac Newton (1642–1727) would draw on Galileo's concepts as he developed his laws of motion and gravity, expressed in Mathematical Principles of Natural Philosophy (1687).

experimental philosophy." The works of Galileo were discussed, and scientists such as mathematician John Wallis, Bishop John Wilkins, and chemist Robert Boyle knew Galileo's work well. Among other Galilean ideas, they studied "the Copernican hypothesis, the satellites of Jupiter, vacuities and nature's abhorrence thereof and the descent of heavy bodies." Wallis said that he appreciated how Galileo had applied "mechanick principles to the solving of philosophical difficulties." In 1638 Wilkins wrote a pro-Copernican book relying heavily on Galileo's work. It was called *The Discovery of a World in the Moone*, and it claimed "that 'tis probable there may be another habitable world in that planet." He wrote it anonymously—even a bishop in Protestant England had to be a little careful about challenging the authorities.

In 1664, young Isaac Newton was shown a translation of Galileo's *Two Chief World Systems* by his tutor at Cambridge, Isaac Barrow. Barrow thought Galileo "one of those moderns resembling and nearly equaling the ancients in sagacity." Newton is, of course, famous for his grand "Law of Universal Gravitation," which explained the speeds and paths not only of projectiles but also of the planets. Newton showed that an object such as the moon, far from the Earth, obeyed the same rules in its orbit as the flight of a cricket ball just above the ground.

Newton read Galileo's arguments for the motion of the Earth. One of these, mentioned earlier, was about the path of a weight dropped from a tower. Historians think it is likely that this argument set Newton thinking whether the moon could also be thought of as a projectile "falling" around the Earth. Newton even used some of Galileo's figures for the calculation. The moon turned out to be rather a good projectile. Although Descartes was the first to formulate a clear definition of inertia, Newton probably got his first feeling for this vital concept from the writings of Galileo.

Newton's "Law of Universal Gravitation" was the final nail in the coffin of the Earth-centered universe, but it was not until the nineteenth century that any experiments could show that the Earth really did move. Astronomers looked for the effect of "parallax." An observer positioned on the Earth as it moves around the sun can be compared to a person looking out of the window of a moving train. In the same way that nearby trees move against the background of those

Léon Foucault's pendulum experiment in the Pantheon in 1851 showed that the Earth rotated, just as Galileo said. Today, the Foucault Pendulum is still on display in Paris.

further away, so nearer stars should move against the background of more distant stars. German astronomer Friedrich Bessel succeeded in measuring this very small parallax effect, and he published his results in 1838.

In 1851 Léon Foucault demonstrated the daily rotation of the Earth in another experiment. He hung a very long pendulum from the roof of the Pantheon in Paris. He swung it slightly. As the day progressed, the direction of swing of the pendulum changed. It was not the pendulum that had rotated, but the Earth beneath it. Galileo would have been pleased—his belief in the motion of the Earth had been supported by both experimentation and by mathematics.

 TEXT-DEPENDENT QUESTIONS

1. What former pupil visited Galileo in 1641, a few months before his death?
2. What did Galileo try to reduce all problems to?
3. What European country had many scientists who admired Galileo's methods?

 RESEARCH PROJECT

Using your school library or the internet, do some research on Isaac Newton and his theories of motion and gravitation. How did he draw on Galileo's work in developing these theories? Explain your findings in a two-page paper and share it with your class.

A bronze statue of Galileo on the façade of the National Library in Florence. The inscription says, "Toward a straighter path."

A PIV·DIRITTO CAMMINO

GALILEO DIAL. MASS. SIST. VII. 42

Chronology

1564

Born in Pisa, Italy, on February 15.

1581

Enrolls at the University of Pisa to study medicine.

1585

Leaves Pisa without a degree. Teaches mathematics privately.

1589

Becomes Professor of Mathematics at the University of Pisa.

1592

Moves to Padua University, again taking a position as Professor of Mathematics.

1597

Writes to German mathematician and astronomer Johannes Kepler about his belief in the Copernican system.

1599

Meets Marina Gamba of Florence. Over the next eleven years, the unmarried couple have three illegitimate children: Virginia (born 1600), Livia (born 1601), and Vincenzio (born 1606).

1602–09

Performs his most important work on motion. Experiments with inclined planes.

c. 1603

Catches severe chill. Suffers from attacks of rheumatism throughout the rest of his life as a result.

1609

Succeeds in improving the newly invented telescope. Begins observations of the skies, particularly Earth's moon and the planet Jupiter.

1610

Announces his discoveries in *The Starry Messenger*. Patronage by Duke of Tuscany. Leaves Padua for Florence.

1612

Engages in correspondence with Jesuit astronomers over the phenomena of sunspots, which indicates imperfections in the sun.

1613

Letters on Sunspots published by the Accademia dei Lincei. The book contains Galileo's first published mention of the principle of inertia, and of his Copernican beliefs.

1616

Instructed by the Roman Catholic Church not to "hold, teach, or defend" the Copernican view.

1623

In August, Maffeo Barberini is elected Pope Urban VIII.

1624

Pope Urban VIII grants Galileo permission to write a book comparing the Tychonic and Copernican cosmologies.

1632

Dialogue Concerning the Two Chief World Systems is published in February. Galileo is summoned to Rome in October to face trial for heresy.

1633

Sentenced to life imprisonment. Later exiled to Siena, and finally kept under house arrest at his villa outside Florence.

1634

Daughter Virginia dies. Galileo continues studying motion.

1637

Becomes blind.

1638

Discourses and Mathematical Demonstrations Relating to Two New Sciences published in Leiden, Holland. It is Galileo's final book, and covers most of his work in physics over the previous thirty years.

1642

Dies on January 9 at Arcetri, Florence.

A statue of Galileo at Padua, Italy. In the background is the Roman Catholic abbey and basilica of Saint Giustina.

Further Reading

Bauer, Susan Wise. *The Story of Western Science: From the Writings of Aristotle to the Big Bang Theory*. New York: W. W. Norton, 2015.

Bynum, William. *A Little History of Science*. New Haven, Conn.: Yale University Press, 2012.

Dolnick, Edward. *The Clockwork Universe: Isaac Newton, the Royal Society, and the Birth of the Modern World*. New York: Harper Perennial, 2012.

Galilei, Galileo. *The Essential Galileo*. Ed. and trans. by Maurice A. Finocchiaro. Indianapolis: Hackett Publishing Co., 2008.

Heilbron, John L. *Galileo*. New York: Oxford University Press, 2012.

Scotti, Dom Pascal. *Galileo Revisited: the Galileo Affair in Context*. San Francisco: Ignatius Press, 2017.

Wotton, David. *Galileo: Watcher of the Skies*. New Haven, Conn.: Yale University Press, 2010.

Statue of Galileo at the Uffizi Gallery in Florence, Italy.

GALILEO GALILEI

GALILÆI GALILÆI LYNCEI
Dialogi, tam eos quos edidit
DE SYSTEMATE MUNDI
quam quos
DE MOTU LOCALI.

Internet Resources

http://galileo.rice.edu

Website of the Galileo Project at Rice University, a source of information on the life of Galileo and on science in his time.

https://www.physics.org

This website from the Institute of Physics is intended to provide resources about physics to students of all ages.

http://www.pbs.org/wgbh/nova

The website of NOVA, a science series that airs on PBS. The series produces in-depth science programming on a variety of topics, from the latest breakthroughs in technology to the deepest mysteries of the natural world.

http://www.biology4kids.com/files/studies_scimethod.html

A simple explanation of the scientific method is available at this website for young people.

http://www.livescience.com

The website Live Science is regularly updated with articles on scientific topics and new developments or discoveries.

Opposite page: This is the frontispiece illustration from an edition of Galileo's Dialogue Concerning the Two Chief World Systems. *This Latin translation of the book was published during the late 1630s. The illustration depicts Aristotle (seated), Ptolemy (center), and Nicolaus Copernicus.*

Series Glossary of Key Terms

anomaly—something that differs from the expectations generated by an established scientific idea. Anomalous observations may inspire scientists to reconsider, modify, or come up with alternatives to an accepted theory or hypothesis.

evidence—test results and/or observations that may either help support or help refute a scientific idea. In general, raw data are considered evidence only once they have been interpreted in a way that reflects on the accuracy of a scientific idea.

experiment—a scientific test that involves manipulating some factor or factors in a system in order to see how those changes affect the outcome or behavior of the system.

hypothesis—a proposed explanation for a fairly narrow set of phenomena, usually based on prior experience, scientific background knowledge, preliminary observations, and logic.

natural world—all the components of the physical universe, as well as the natural forces at work on those things.

objective—to consider and represent facts without being influenced by biases, opinions, or emotions. Scientists strive to be objective, not subjective, in their reasoning about scientific issues.

observe—to note, record, or attend to a result, occurrence, or phenomenon.

science—knowledge of the natural world, as well as the process through which that knowledge is built through testing ideas with evidence gathered from the natural world.

subjective—referring to something that is influenced by biases, opinions, and/or emotions. Scientists strive to be objective, not subjective, in their reasoning about scientific issues.

test—an observation or experiment that could provide evidence regarding the accuracy of a scientific idea. Testing involves figuring out what one would expect to observe if an idea were correct and comparing that expectation to what one actually observes.

theory—a broad, natural explanation for a wide range of phenomena in science. Theories are concise, coherent, systematic, predictive, and broadly applicable, often integrating and generalizing many hypotheses. Theories accepted by the scientific community are generally strongly supported by many different lines of evidence. However, theories may be modified or overturned as new evidence is discovered.

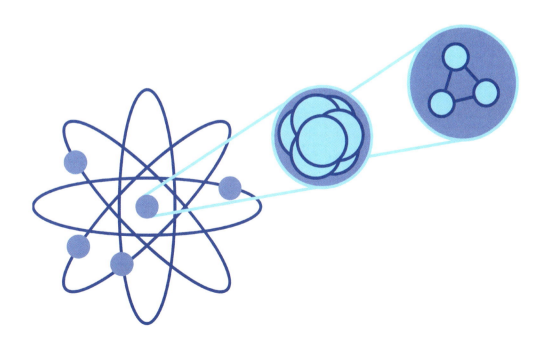

Statue of Galileo on a street in Barcelona, Spain.

Index

About the Author

Mary Steffanelli earned an M.Sc. in the history of science at Oxford University, and has conducted research in physics, astronomy, and mathematics. She currently works at the Science Museum in South Kensington, London.

Photo Credits

Everett Historical: 18, 52, 88; Library of Congress: 23; Mathematical Association of America: 60; National Aeronautics and Space Administration: 36; used under license from Shutterstock, Inc.: 9, 14, 27, 38, 49, 64, 65, 85, 87; Brendan Howard / shutterstock.com: 77; Dragan Jovanovic / shutterstock.com: 92; Vladimir Korostyshevskiy / shutterstock.com: 15; Viacheslav Lopatin / shutterstock.com: 72; PitK / shutterstock.com: 20; Tupungato / shutterstock.com: 80; zummolo / shutterstock.com: 82; Wellcome Library: 1, 6, 16, 25, 30, 32, 33, 35, 42, 46, 54, 56, 61, 68, 70, 75, 78; Wikimedia Commons: 13, 28, 40, 45, 59, 66.